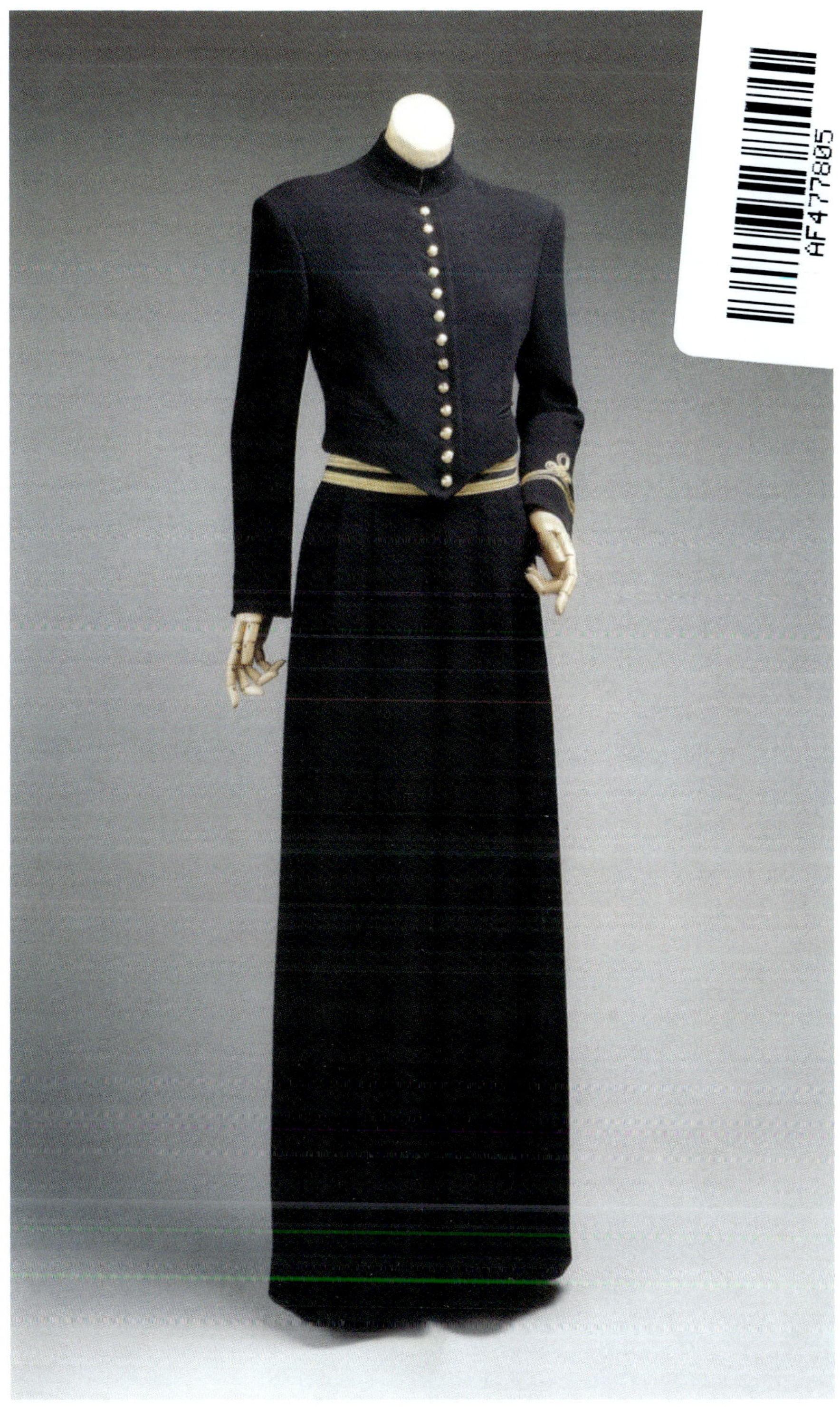

FIGURE 1. Ralph Lauren. Spencer suit, spring/summer 1990

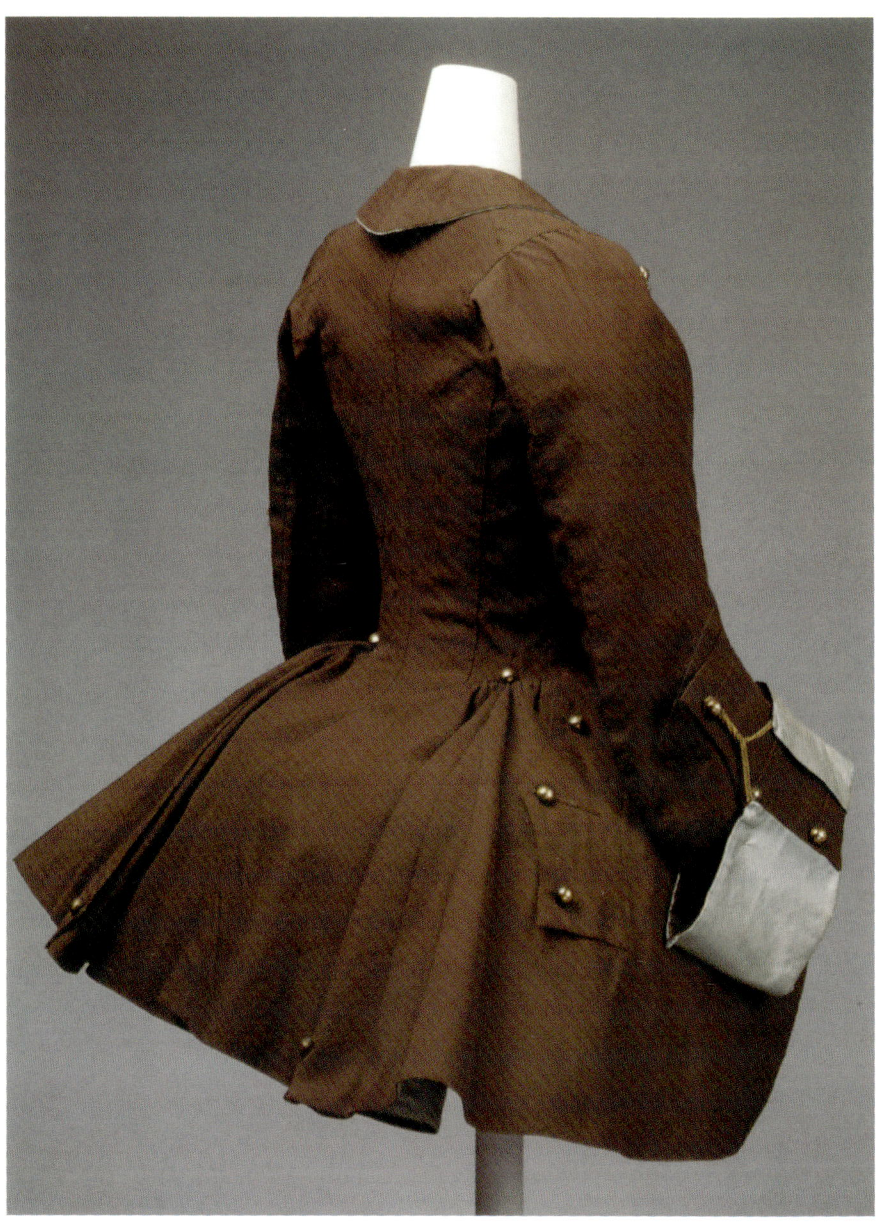

FIGURE 2. English. Riding coat, 1775

The elements of military dress, with their genesis in function, have become the decorative lexicon of modern attire, although all performed as embellishment long after their first conscripted function. Epaulets once protected shoulder and arm and ball buttons could be used as shot in battle, and sabretaches anchored the saber and served as detachable pockets.

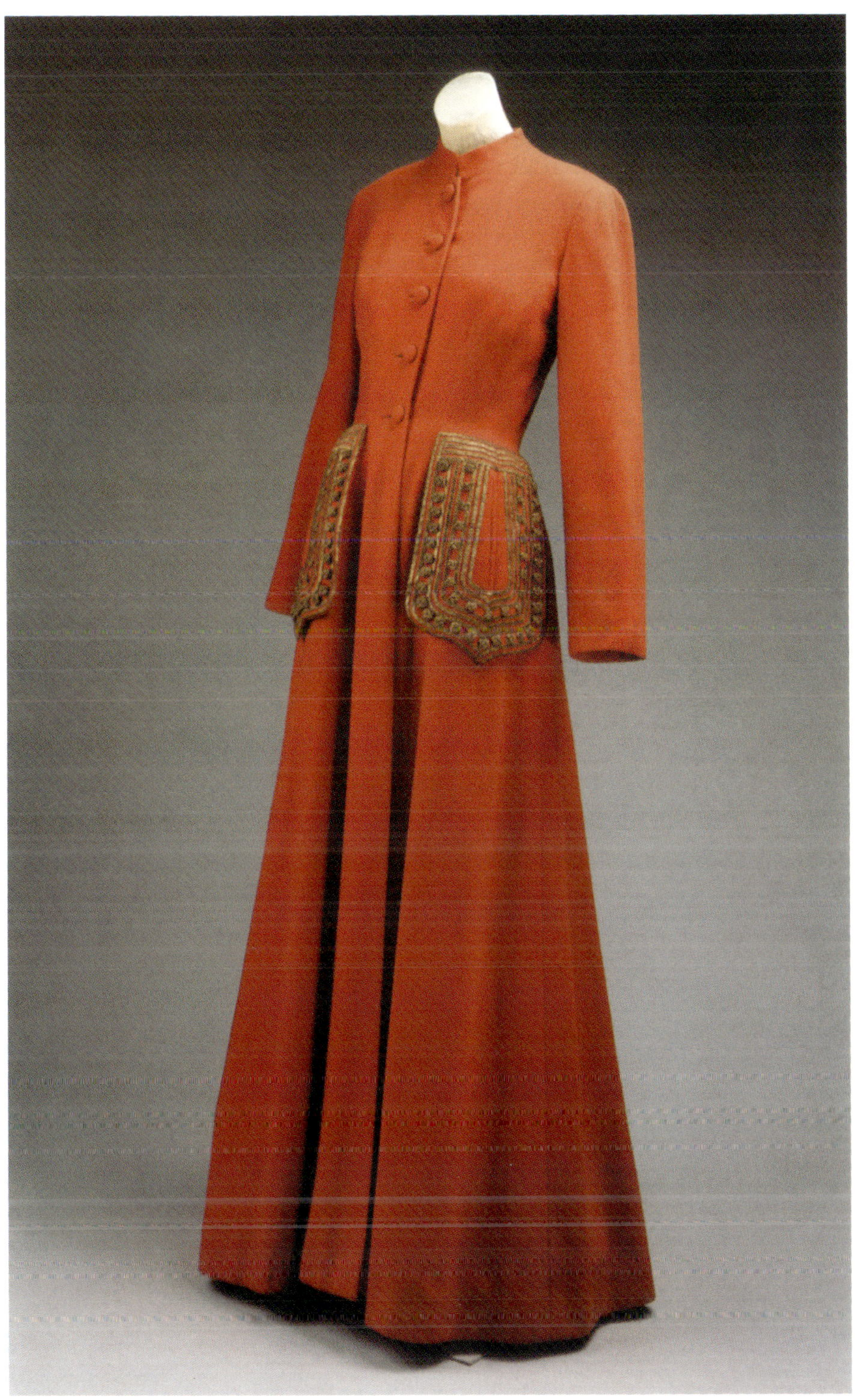

FIGURE 3. Bruno. Evening coat, 1947

SWORDS INTO PLOUGHSHARES

RICHARD MARTIN

AND

HAROLD KODA

THE METROPOLITAN MUSEUM OF ART

NEW YORK

INTRODUCTION

In Stendhal's novel of modern resolution, *The Red and the Black*, Julien Sorel is faced with choosing between the black cassock of the clergy and the valorous red of Napoleon's soldiers. Sorel makes a rueful choice of the black, but his sartorial decision is the matrix of a very modern conflict between passion and the social order. The style of the military has enchanted the modern imagination. Despite the waste manifest in war, modern culture has realized its belligerent, aggressive style as an option tinged with sentiments of courage and honor. Stephen Crane's paean to the warrior, *The Red Badge of Courage*, renders war as exceptional intensity and fervor: "Within him, as he hurled himself forward, was born a love, a despairing fondness for this flag which was near him. It was a creation of beauty and invulnerability." War renders heroes; war tenders fortitude. Moreover, war offers a modern wardrobe the efficacy of virtue-imbued, tested, sentimental, epic dress. Again and again, war's fiery raiment has become a figure for modern apparel.

"Swords into Ploughshares" strives neither to bury nor to praise war, but one cannot ignore the impact of the military on modern clothing. Effectively, the military is more than a collective glory: It is the testing ground for the utility and accommodation of clothing that may be brought home into civilian service. The prophecy of Isaiah (2: 4), "They shall beat their swords into ploughshares, and their spears into pruning-hooks: nation shall not lift up sword against nation, neither shall they learn war any more," remains forestalled, but not the demonstrable striving in clothing.

The military origin of modern clothing is often neglected. In such instances as trenchcoats, navy blue or khaki, and the cummerbund, most contemporary wearers are probably not wholly mindful of the military matrix of their clothing selection, but such an obscure iconography does not displace the warrior as source. Instead, it suggests the complexity of clothing genealogy. Yet no contemporary wearer could be unaware of the trenchcoat's aura of protection and its outfitting with many serviceable if dormant elements, or the ship-shape propriety of navy blue, or the exotic aura of the cummerbund and khaki. Does modern life require the shielding of arm and shoulder from saber slashes that occasioned the epaulet? The epaulet has become a detail and adornment of modern dress with its usefulness long defaulted but with an abiding connotation of self-confidence and etiquette. Memories of victory mingle with the pragmatism of war's determination of declarative and defensive clothing, as such apparel is absorbed into modern dress. A legion of concepts from all branches of the military, tested by the quartermaster and proven in utility, have become standards of contemporary costume, including sailors' pea jackets and bell-bottomed trousers, colorful sashes initially worn of necessity to serve as litters to carry the wounded off the field of battle, aviator glasses and bomber (A-2 aviator) jackets, braid—first as chest shield and subsequently decoration, olive drab, Eisenhower jackets, and camouflage, among many other items.

"Uniforms," said Diana Vreeland, "are the sportswear of the nineteenth century." Impeccable tailoring, with provision for strenuous body movement, rank, pomp, and identity, has made uniforms effective as dress. Today, many men and women wear the all-purpose trenchcoat in atrophied memory of its beginnings as an officer's coat in the Boer War and ultimately in World War I.

Fashion critic Suzy Menkes recently has written in the *International Herald Tribune* (May 9, 1995), "Fashion wartime images are often uncomfortable and even unacceptable. There is something terrible and trivial about jackboots and neo-Nazi trenchcoats made 'fashionable' or Sam Brown belts as a 'fun' accessory." Yet war's presence is inexorable, impossible for the socially engaged art of fashion to ignore. Of course, uniforms can stand as signs of savagery and oppression. Is fashion playing dangerous and callous war games or fulfilling Isaiah's vision of crafting fertile ploughshares from sharp swords?

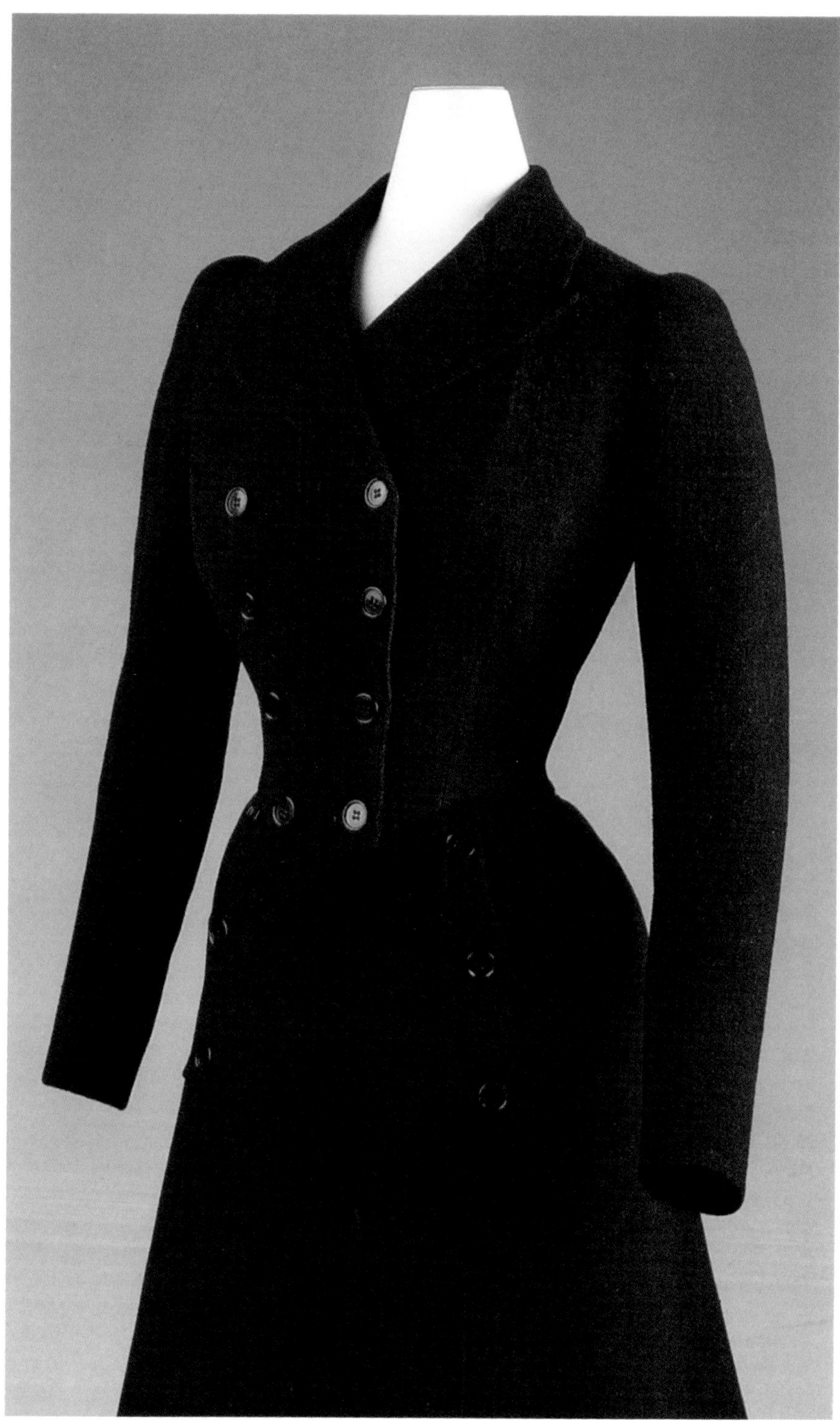

FIGURE 4. American. Suit, ca. 1900

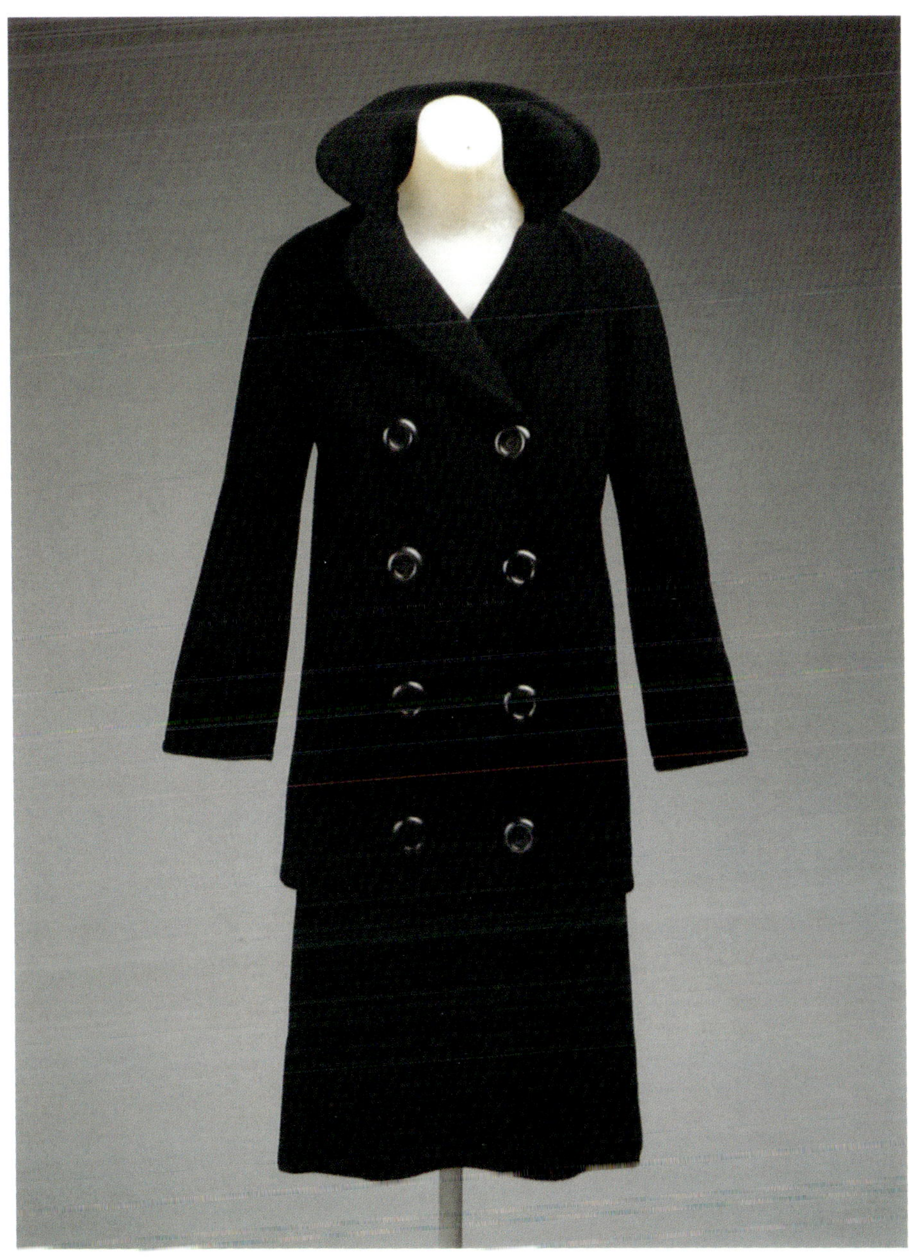

FIGURE 5. Pauline Trigère. Pea jacket ensemble, 1960

Among the civilian forces, none was more romantic than the Navy. Sailors have offered an assortment of adaptable clothes: drop-front and bell-bottomed pants, pea coats, and middy blouses. Even the color "navy" occupies its central position in modern dress from the mettle of the sailor.

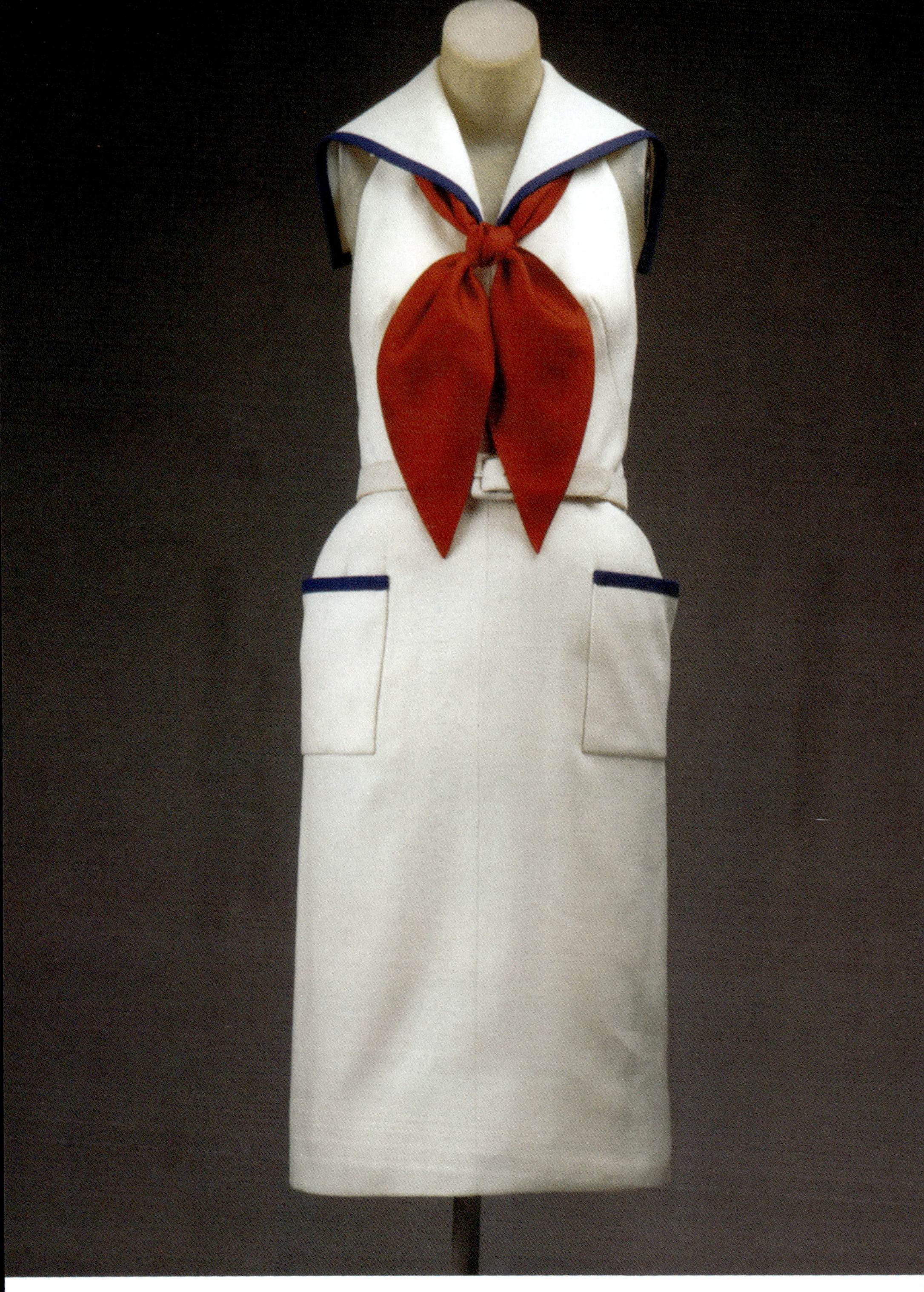

FIGURE 6. Traina-Norell. Summer dress, 1954

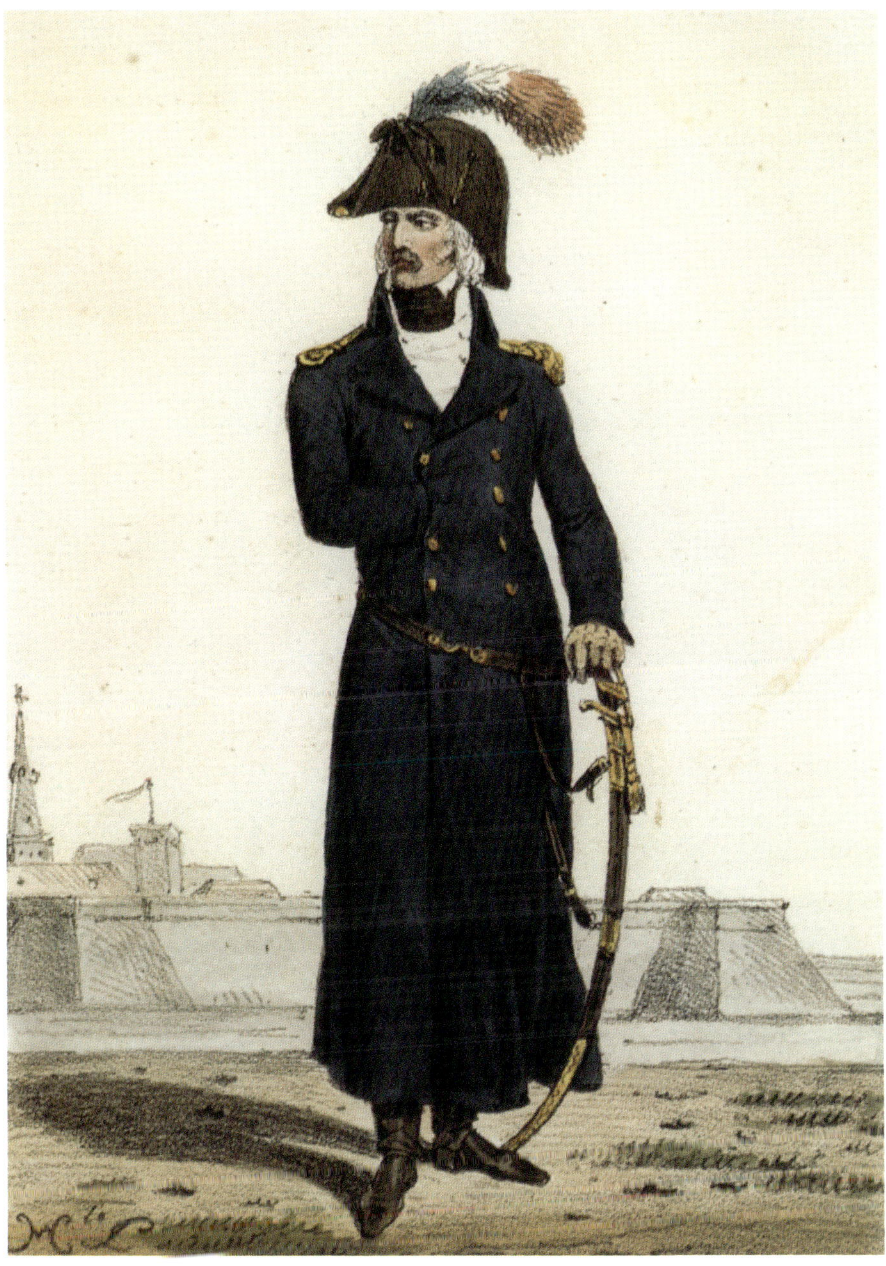

FIGURE 7. Hippolyte Lecomte. "Officier d'Etat Major, en petit uniforme, 1794"

The exposed facings of double-breasted closures evolved into applied trim not only in fashion but in some dress uniforms as well. From the eighteenth century onward, brass buttons came to be associated with the military. In Figure 12, the seed-shaped buttons suggest a double form of the tit button characteristic of Hussar uniforms.

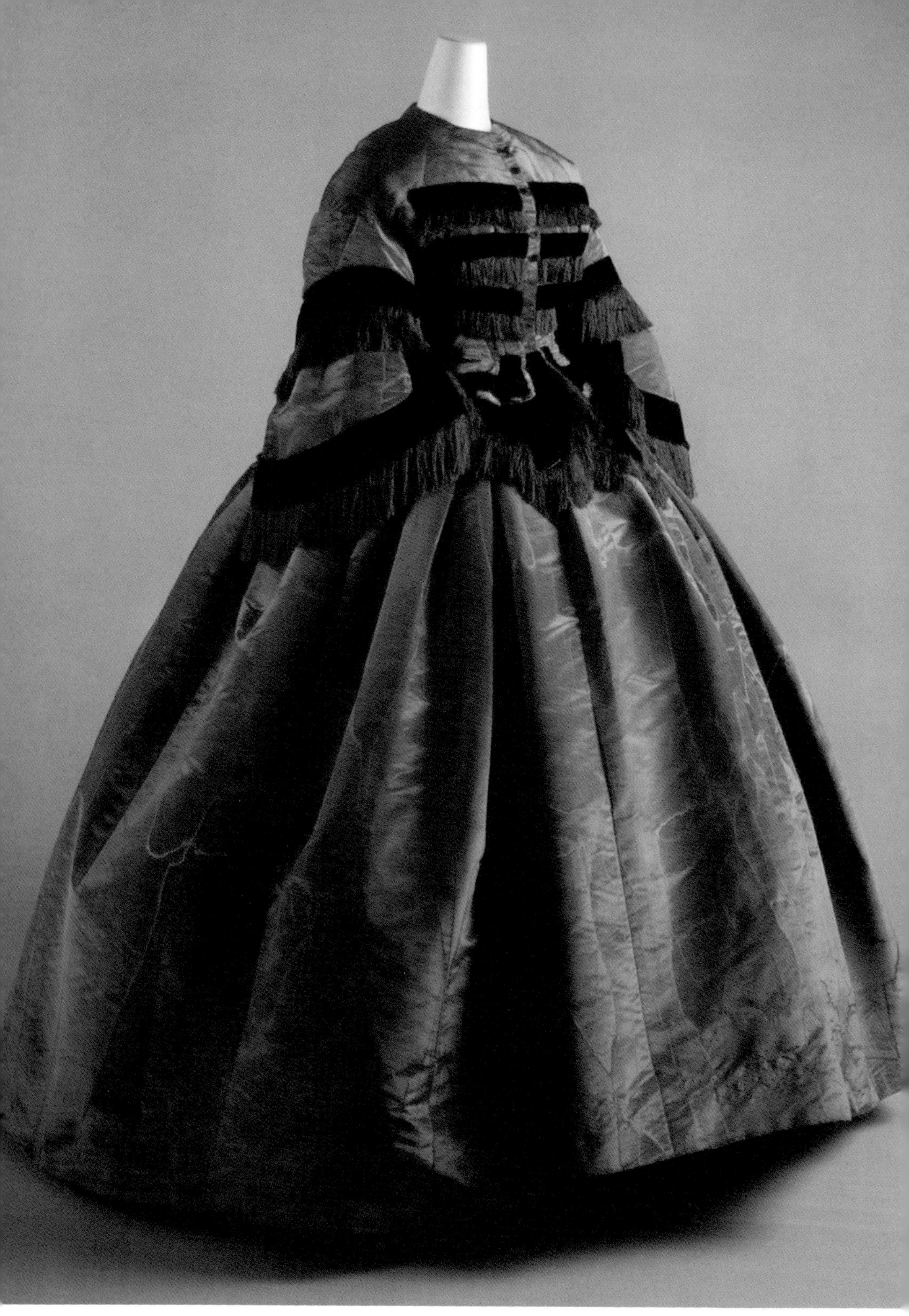

FIGURE 8. American. Day dress, 1858

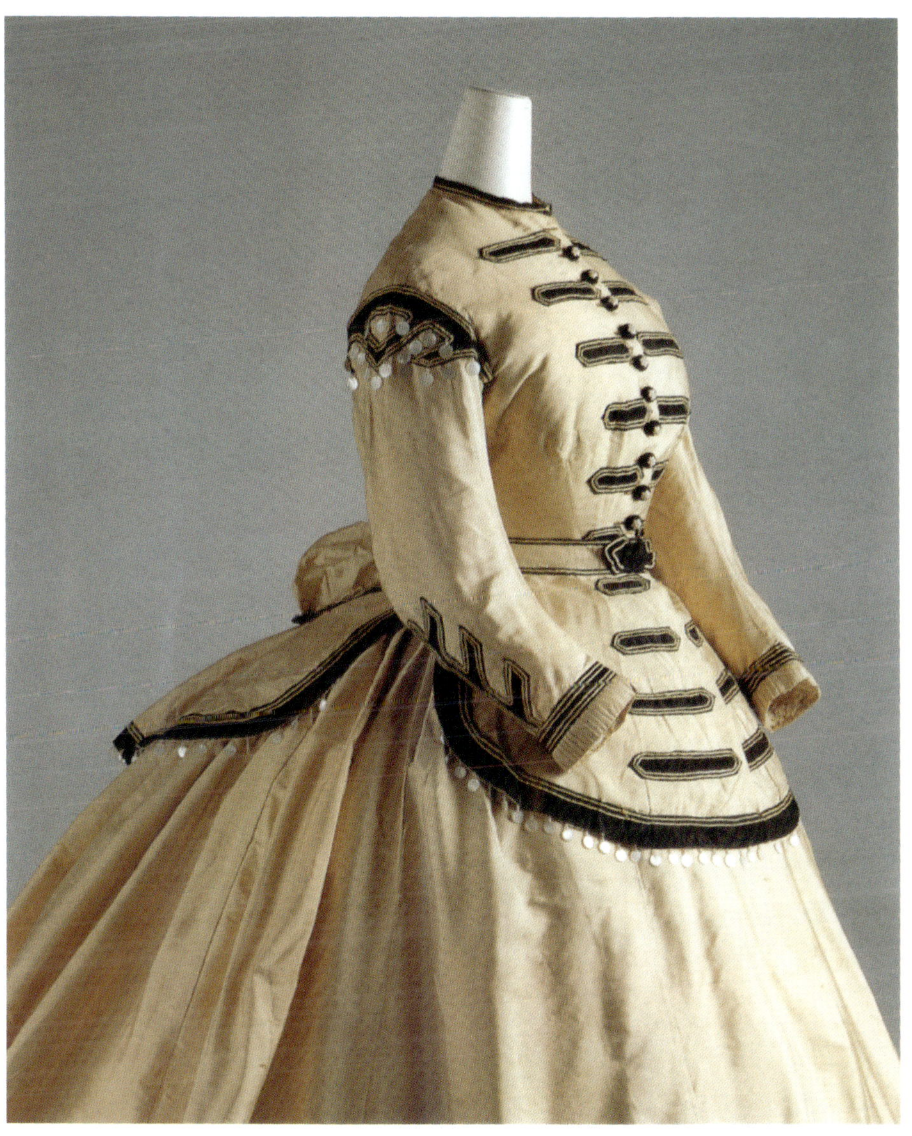

FIGURE 9. American. Day dress, 1860

Braided tabs simulating the closures on eighteenth- and early-nineteenth-century uniforms were popular for walking dresses and tailored outerwear in the nineteenth century. The epic of the civilian soldier was thus emulated on the home front.

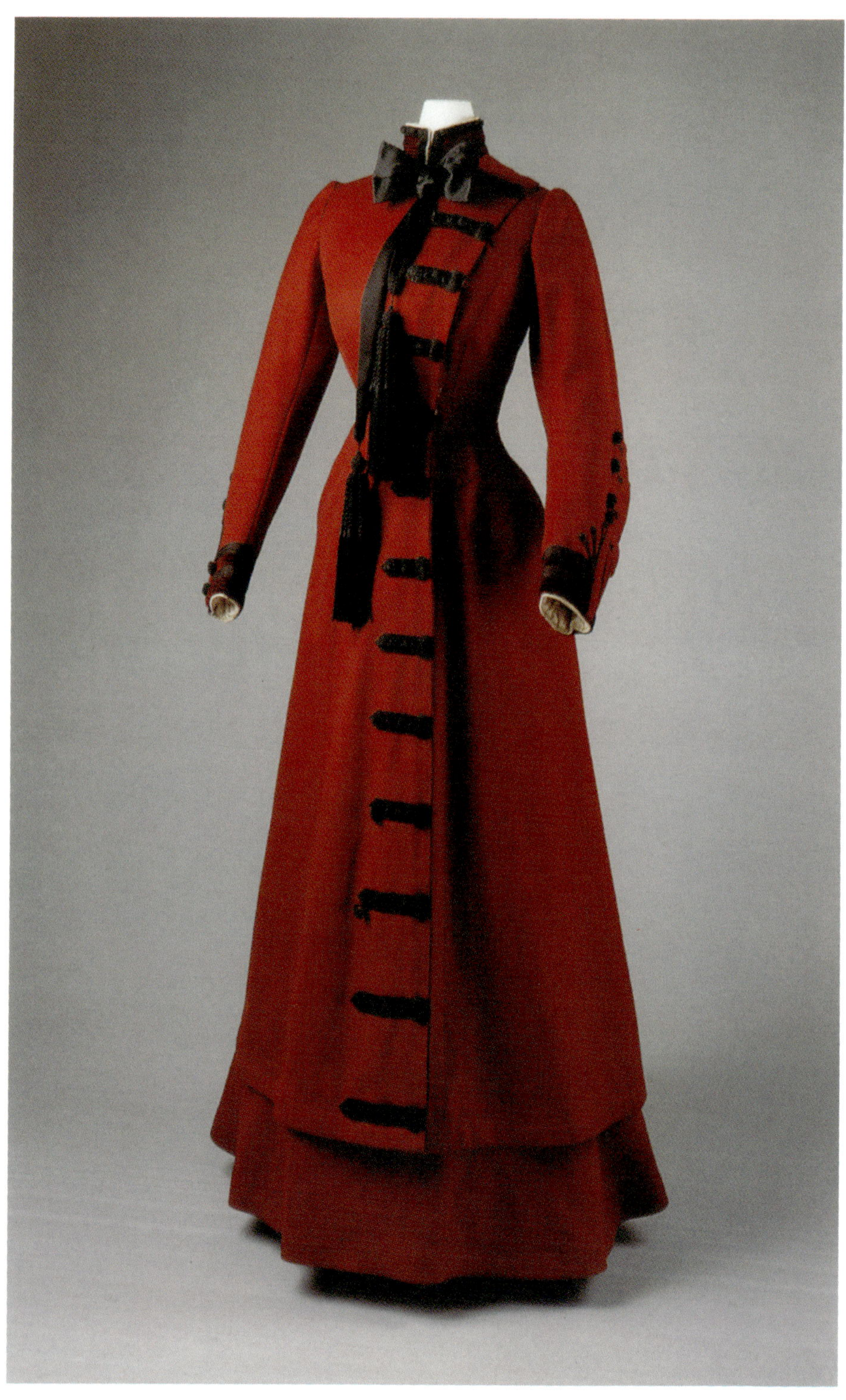

FIGURE 10. French. Coat ensemble, 1902

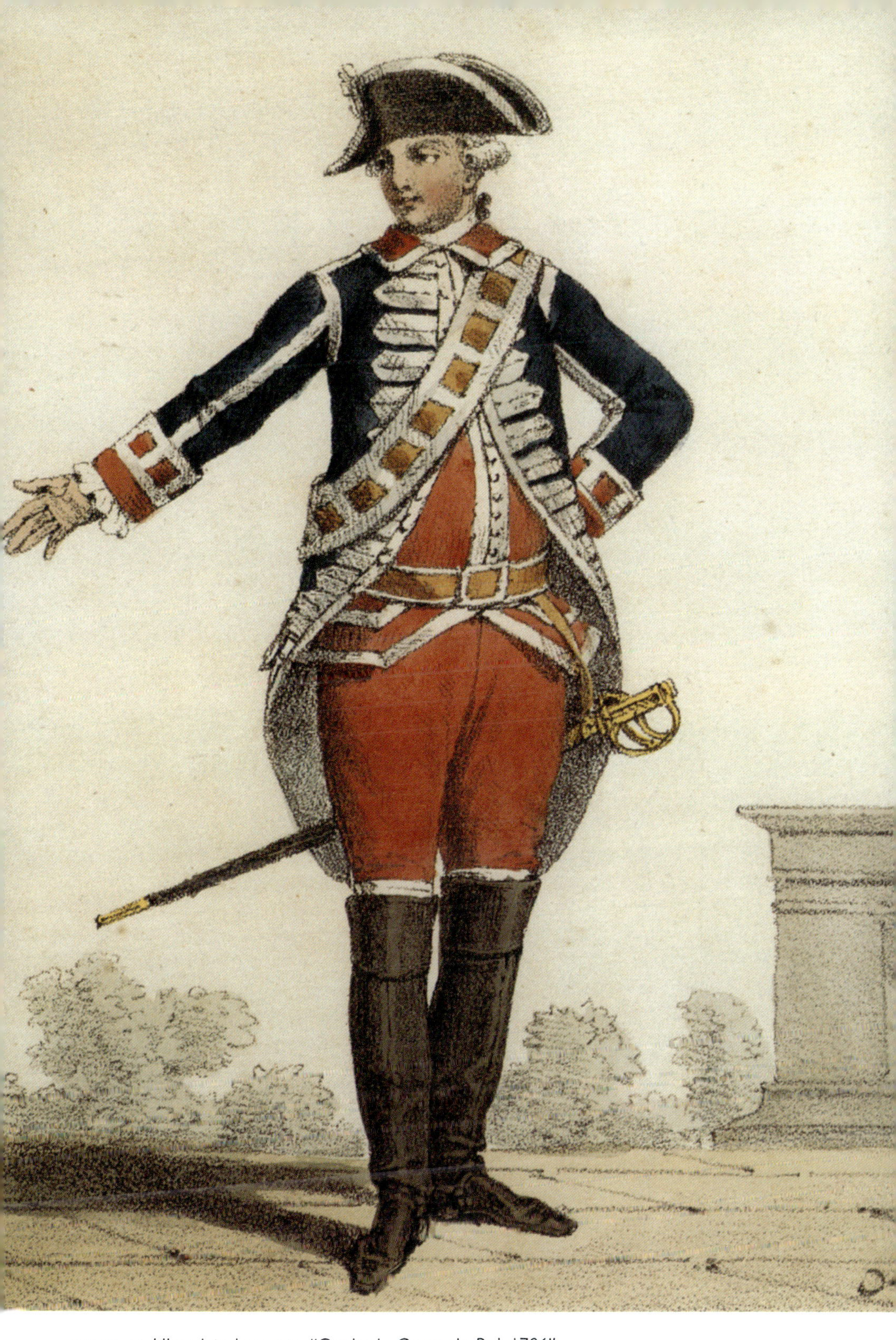

FIGURE 11. Hippolyte Lecomte. "Garde du Corps du Roi, 1786"

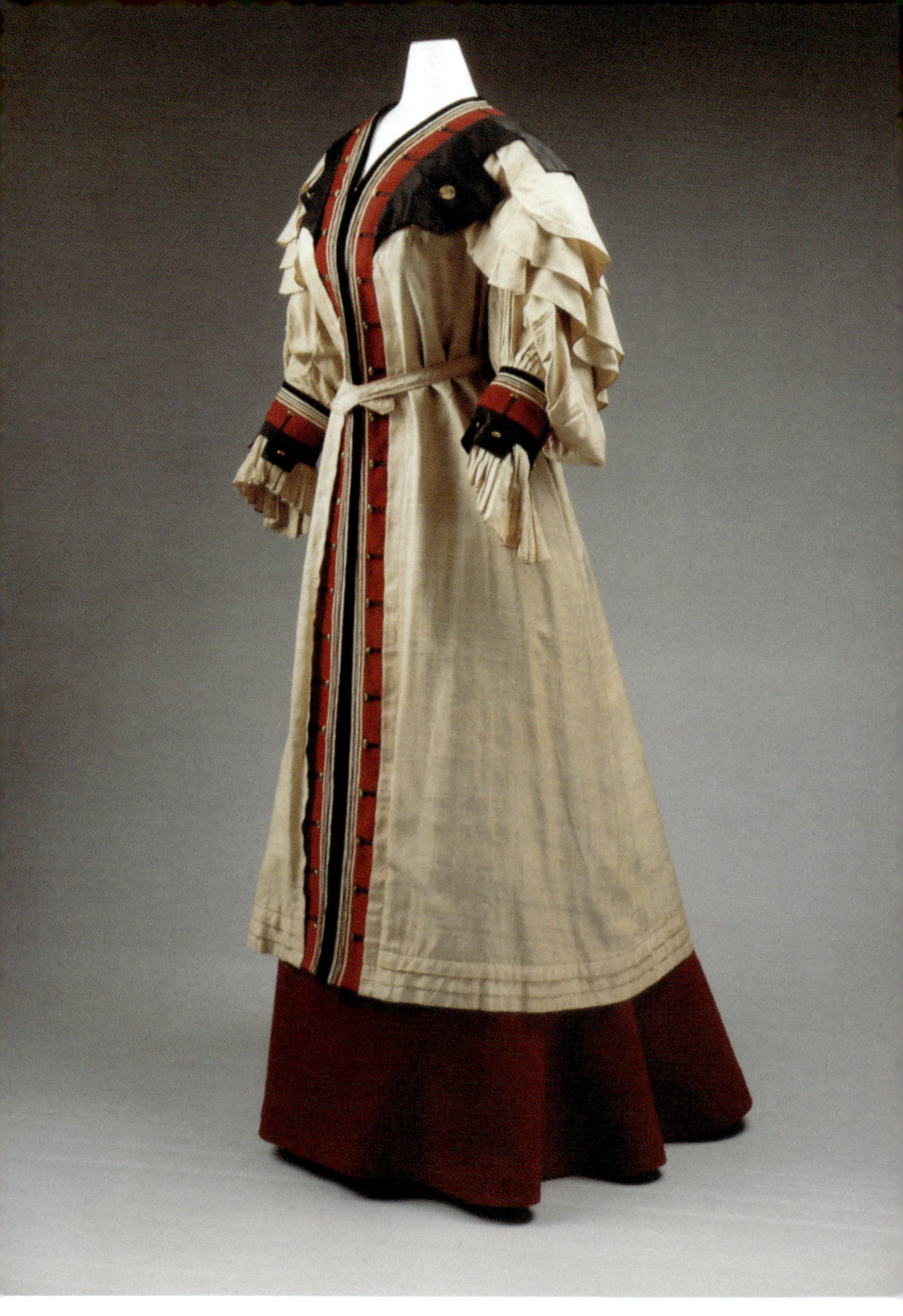

FIGURE 12. American. Coat, 1901–4

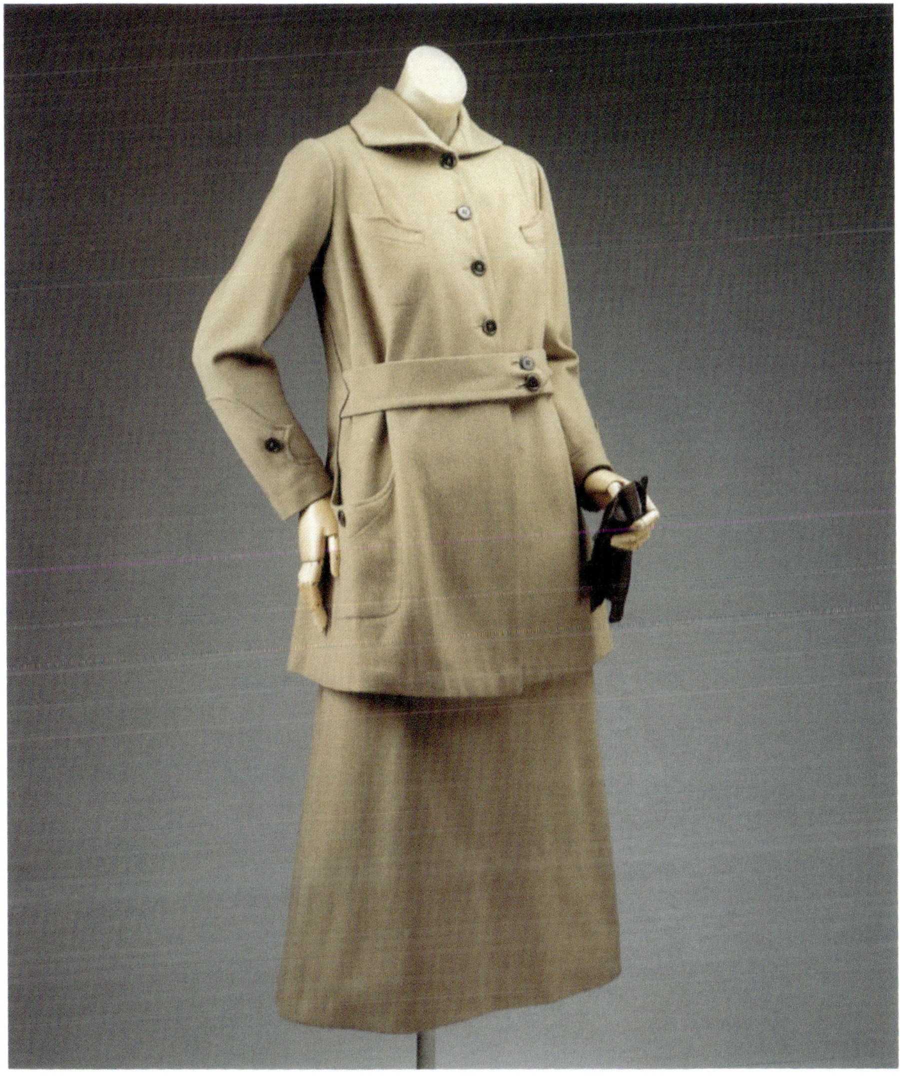

FIGURE 13. American. Suit, 1916

Khaki, introduced by the British in India for its utility in a dusty, hot climate,
has become more associated with the cool supremacy of the English officer
than with its utilitarian matrix as an adaptation of indigenous dress.

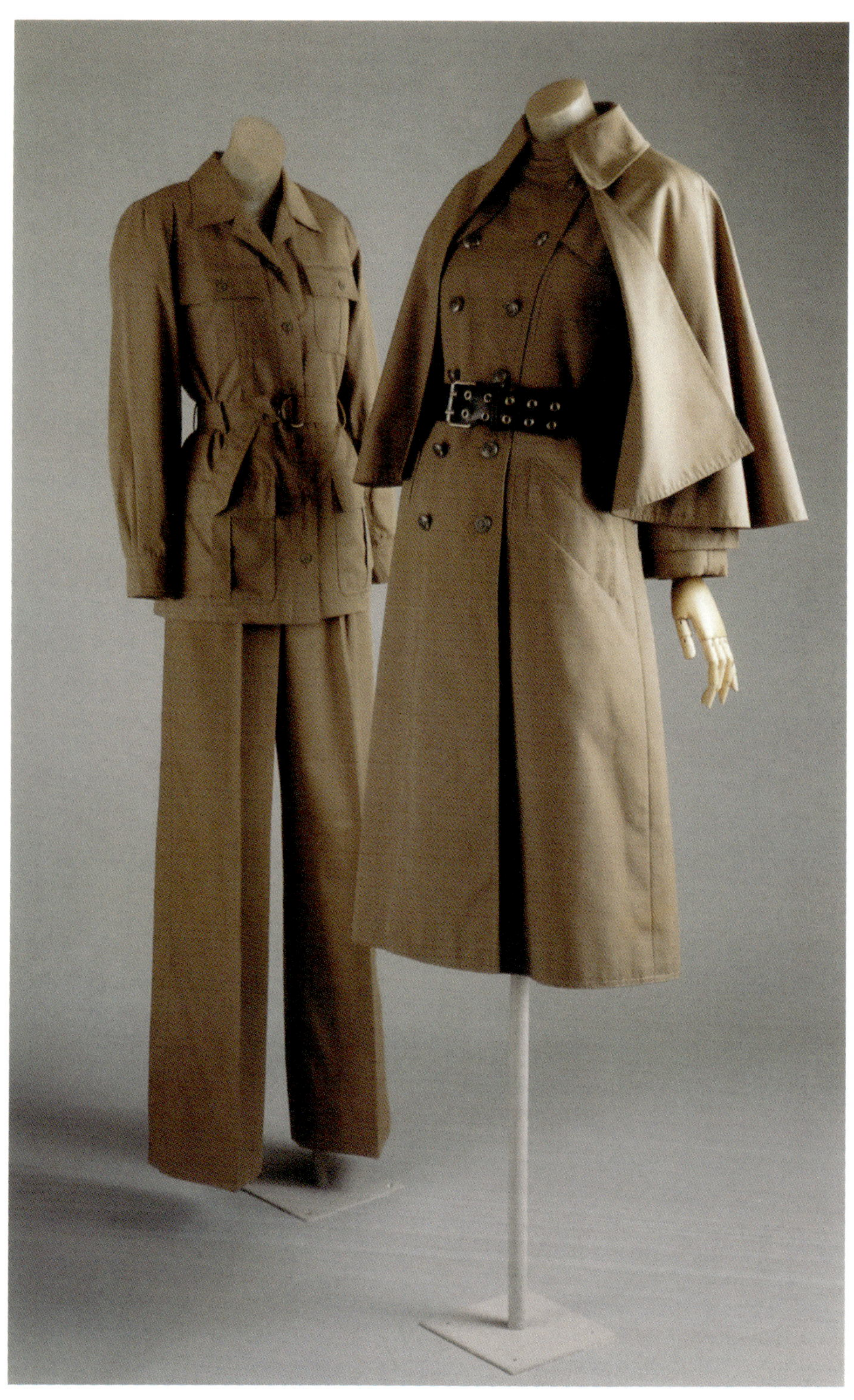

FIGURE 14. (LEFT) Yves Saint Laurent. "Safari" suit, 1970; (RIGHT) Anne Klein. Raincoat, 1971

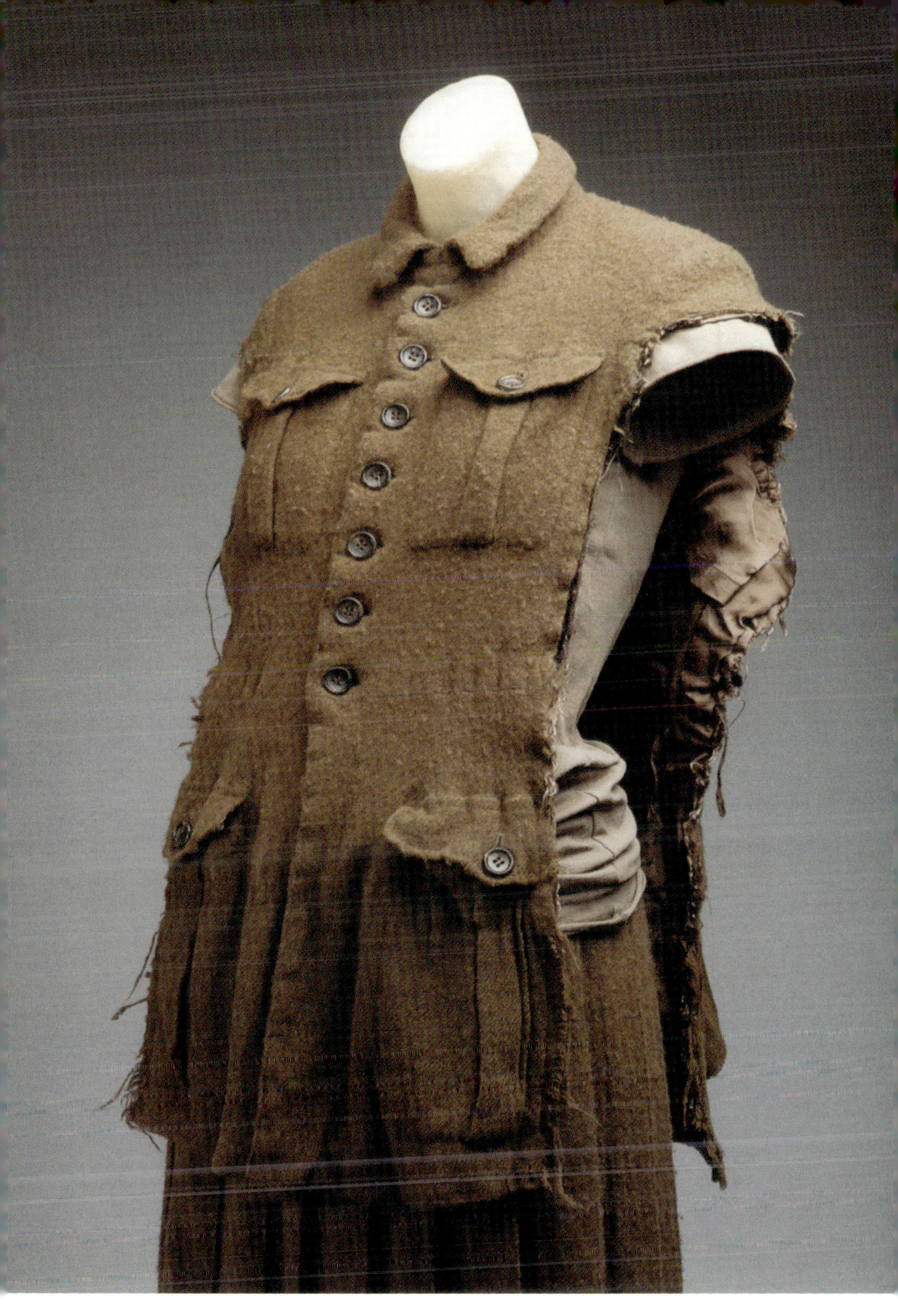

FIGURE 15. Comme des Garçons. Tabard ensemble, fall/winter 1994–95

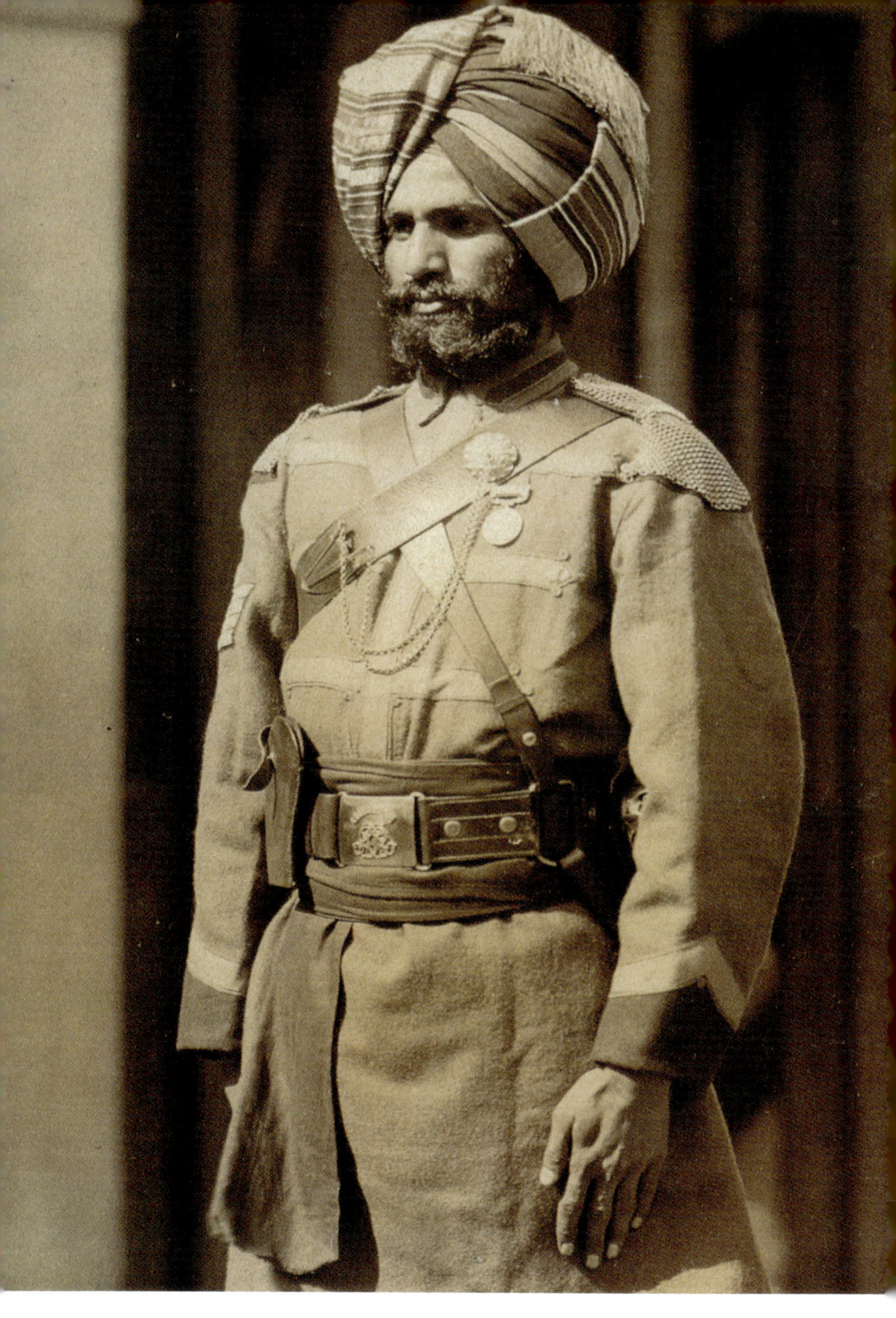

FIGURE 16. Sergeant, The Queen's Own Corps of Guides, Cavalry, ca. 1893

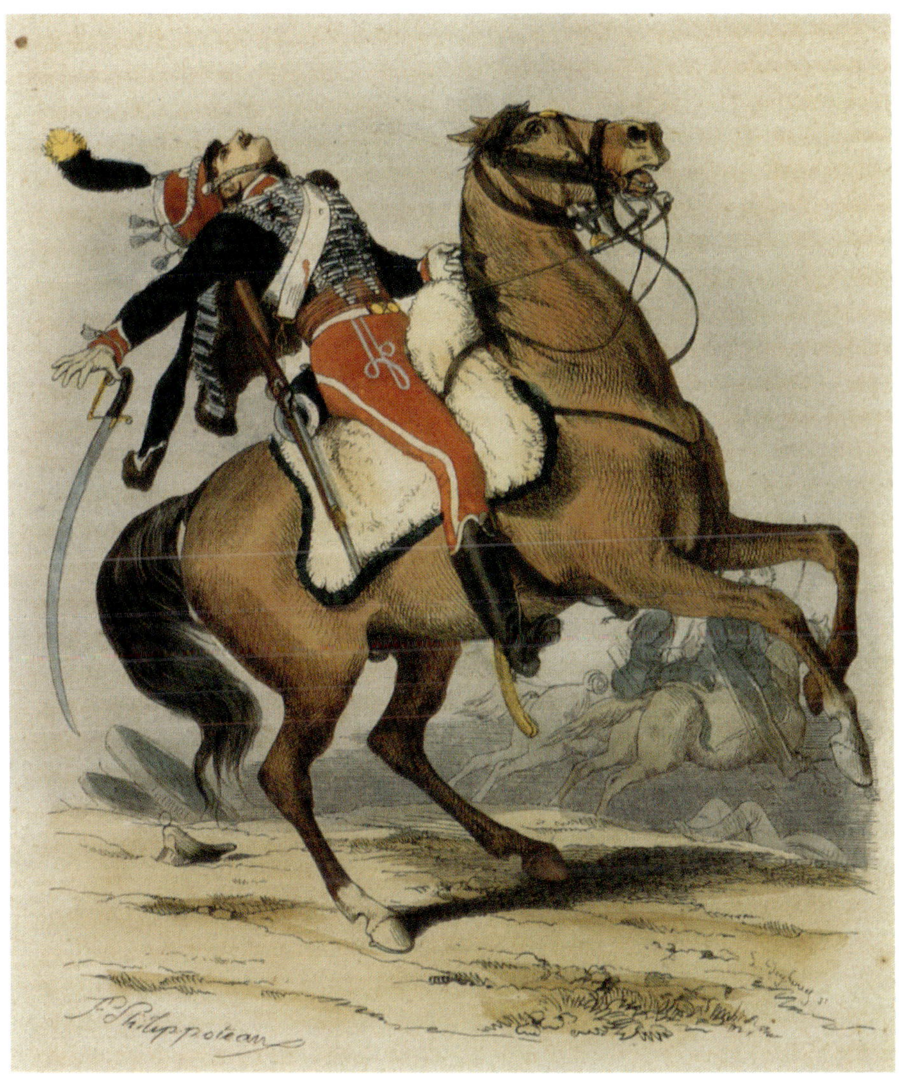

FIGURE 17. "Gardes d'Honneur 3ᵐᵉ Régiment, 1811"

If the braid worn by Hussars and Zouaves began as a layer of protection to deflect sword blades, it quickly became a cipher of estimable decoration, implying both personal status and state service as it was absorbed into apparel ornament.

CAPTIONS

FIGURE 1.
Ralph Lauren. Spencer suit, spring/summer
1990.
Navy blue silk crepe with gold soutache braid.
Courtesy Ralph Lauren

FIGURE 2.
English. Riding coat, 1775.
*Brown goat's hair-and-silk blend with pale blue
silk satin.*
Mr. and Mrs. Alan S. Davis Gift Fund, 1976
(1976.147.2)

FIGURE 3.
Bruno. Evening coat, 1947.
*Red-orange wool with gilt-embroidered
sabretache pockets.*
Gift of Bruno, 1948
(CI 48.9)

FIGURE 4.
American. Suit, ca. 1900.
Navy blue wool.
Gift of the Heirs of Maud Van Cortlandt
Taylor Hill, 1965
(CI 65.30.3a-c)

FIGURE 5.
Pauline Trigère. Pea jacket ensemble, 1960.
Black wool crepe.
Gift of Pauline Trigère, 1993
(1993.138.10a-d)

FIGURE 6.
Traina-Norell. Summer dress, 1954.
*White linen with blue linen trim and
red silk-twill scarf.*
Gift of Mrs. Max M. Fisher, 1977
(1977.279.1a-c)

FIGURE 7.
Hippolyte Lecomte.
"Officier d'Etat Major, en petit uniforme, 1794."
*Costumes Civils et Militaires de la Monarchie
Française depuis 1200 jusqu'à 1820, 1820.*
Gift of Mrs. Sidney Horowitz, 1993

FIGURE 8.
American. Day dress, 1858.
*Green silk moiré with dark green velvet-and-
fringe trim.*
Gift of Henri Bendel II, 1955 (CI 55.1.12a-c)

FIGURE 9.
American. Day dress, 1860.
*Dark cream silk with black silk faille and
mother-of-pearl spangle trim.*
Gift of Mary Pierrepont Beckwith, 1969
(CI 69.33.4a-d)

FIGURE 10.
French. Coat ensemble, 1902.
*Burgundy wool broadcloth with dark red velvet
and black soutache trim.*
Gift of Miss Frances M. Dickinson, 1955
(CI 55.65ab)

FIGURE 11.
Hippolyte Lecomte.
"Garde du Corps du Roi, 1786."
*Costumes Civils et Militaires de la Monarchie
Française depuis 1200 jusqu'à 1820, 1820.*
Gift of Mrs. Sidney Horowitz, 1993

FIGURE 12.
American. Coat, 1901–4.
*Natural colored silk pongee with red wool felt,
black silk taffeta, soutache, and brass-button trim.*
Gift of Mrs. Earl Rowe, 1951 (CI 51.15.3ab)

FIGURE 13.
American. Suit, 1916.
Tan wool twill.
Irene Lewisohn Bequest, 1951 (CI 51.97.26a-c)

FIGURE 14.
(LEFT) Yves Saint Laurent. "Safari" suit, 1970.
Khaki cotton twill.
Gift of Barbara and Gregory Reynolds, 1984
(1984.598.96a-c)
(RIGHT) Anne Klein. Raincoat, 1971.
Khaki cotton canvas.
Gift of M. N. Rubinstein, 1977 (1977.362.33a-e)

FIGURE 15.
Comme des Garçons.
Tabard ensemble, fall/winter 1994–95.
Dark khaki milled wool.
Courtesy Comme des Garçons

FIGURE 16.
Sergeant, The Queen's Own Corps of Guides,
Cavalry, ca. 1893.
Courtesy Dervis Historical Research, New York

FIGURE 17.
"Gardes d'Honneur, 3me Régiment, 1814."
Gift of Mrs. Eva Rosencrans, 1967

FIGURE 18.
American. Suit, 1892.
Black wool serge with soutache trim.
Gift of Mrs. William R. Witherell, 1953
(CI 53.72.9a-c)

FRONT COVER.
British Painter, Unknown.
*Major Hubert Gillies, 1st Duke of York's Own
Lancers (Skinner's Horse), ca. 1920.
Oil on canvas.*
From the collection, CAVALRY ROAD, of
Christopher Ross.
Photograph courtesy Konstantin

BACK COVER.
Stephen Sprouse. Man's suit, 1988.
*Red, blue, orange, and yellow "camouflage"
printed cotton.*
Gift of Michael Macko, 1991 (1991.35.1ab)

Battle yields some inevitable rewards in the
cummerbund, epaulet, braid, and camouflage
put to civilian use with an alacrity and a
pacification that bespeaks clothing's significant
aesthetic and social roles.

This publication has been issued in conjunction with the exhibition "Swords into Ploughshares"
held at The Metropolitan Museum of Art, New York, from September 7 to November 27, 1995.

Published by The Metropolitan Museum of Art, New York
Copyright ©1995 by The Metropolitan Museum of Art, New York
All rights reserved.
Printed in the United States of America
ISBN 0-87099-757-2

John P. O'Neill, Editor in Chief
Ellen Shultz, Editor
Tsang Seymour Design Studio, Designer
Matthew Pimm, Production Manager

Photographs by Karin Willis, The Photograph Studio, The Metropolitan Museum of Art,
unless otherwise noted.

ISBN POD edition: 978-0-300-20136-9
Printer/binder POD edition: Acme Bookbinding, Charlestown, MA

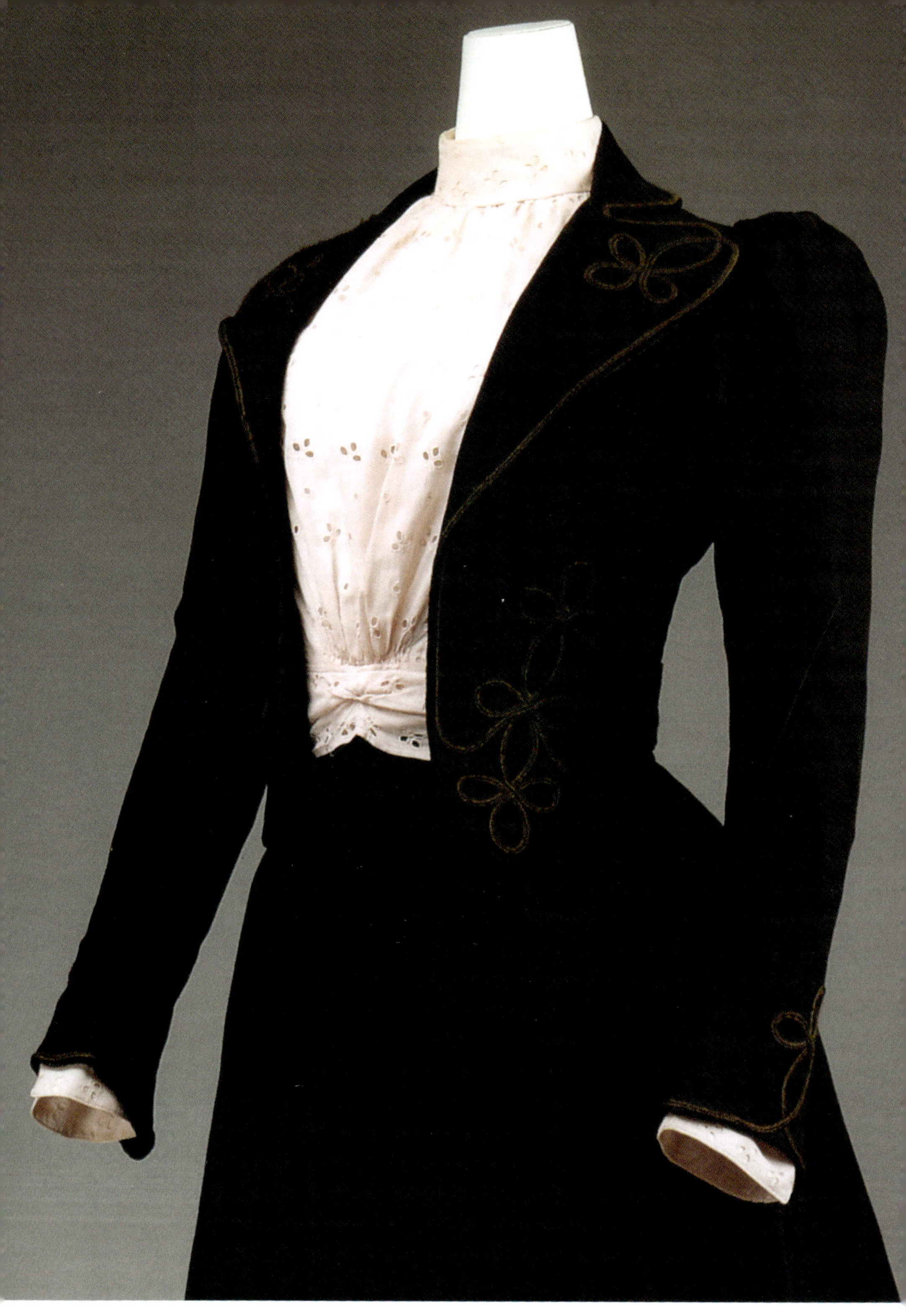

FIGURE 18. American. Suit, 1892

ISBN 9780300201369